VIRGINIA SATIR

MEDITATIONS & INSPIRATIONS

CELESTIALARTS

A special note of appreciation to Henry Harder for the diligent help in transcribing, editing and organizing some of the material in this book.

Celestial Arts
P.O. Box 7327
Berkeley, California 94707

Design by Ken Scott
Cover photo by Barbara Dorsey
Printed in the U.S.A.

Library of Congress Cataloging-in-Publication Data

Satir, Virginia M.
  Meditations.

  1. Meditation. 2. Meditations. I. Banmen, John. II. Gerber, Jane.
III. Title.
BL627.S375 1985   158'.12   85-13302

      4 5 6 — 93 92 91 90

Three

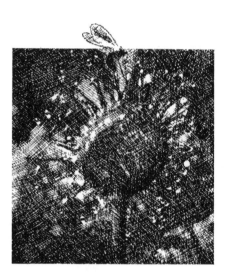

I remembered the many
times when a particular book read at a time
when I was in a receiving mood, opened up
new possibilities which resulted in my taking
new directions for myself. . . .

Virginia Satir

CHOICE

Clasp your hands . . .
Feel the energy flow.
Let yourself feel that connection,
the energy that moves around.
Put yourself where you've always been,
in the universal life-force.
Very gently bring your hands to rest
in your lap.
Breathing comfortably, tell yourself:
"I am a life form based in divinity.
I am able to see,
to hear,
to feel,
to smell,
to touch,
to move,
to speak,

to *choose*."

Virginia Satir

Meditations & Inspirations

YOUR UNIVERSAL PARTS

Become aware of your universal parts, which
can be talked about
as if
they were alone,
but
cannot be lived without being
in touch with every single one.

Be aware that you are a veritable beehive of activity and
that excitement begins when
you begin to know
and can find
how
these various parts
integrate.

Which ones have you been fighting?
Which ones have been sleeping?
Which ones have you felt to be dangerous or
ignored?
Which one has been so totally acceptable to you that
you wanted it to be your only
part?

Just be aware.
Each person's discovery is going to be
unique.
Yet
there will be
some
similarities.

See it in your body.
You tingle with the idea that you are a
symphony.
You are an art piece.
You are unique,
unlike anyone else, yet
created out of the same colors of the rainbow.

READY FOR LEARNING

Begin now to be in touch with your breathing. Adjust your body so it feels comfortable. Let yourself become prepared. Ask the part of yourself that takes in information and new experiences to allow you to be relaxed and open. Remember, as you hear and see, to let things come in. Taste them and allow them to be swallowed when your inside says they fit.

At this moment, could you allow yourself to *remember that you have lived successfully so far?* The way is open for you to add to yourself. Could you allow yourself to be aware that there is so much about a human being, and about human beings together on this planet in the universe, from which we can learn?

We can learn what we need in abundance, and to be happy, productive, respected human beings. That we may not be fully there does not mean we don't have the ability, only that we haven't found it and learned how to use it yet. Everyone has this human potential.

Virginia Satir   *Meditations & Inspirations*

Give a message of love to your left brain. Make it a strong message of love, because your left hemisphere doesn't know yet that your right hemisphere will help you in your learnings.

Allow yourself now, with your eyes open, to feel that body of yours—that gorgeous temple, that magnificent miracle. Ease into your seat in a balanced way, making sure both feet are on the floor. If there are any little tight places as you take in your breath, send the breath through your body. Stop to smile when you find a tight place and let the tensions leave on an outgoing breath.

Notice that, whether you are aware of it or not, your breath is coming and going. As you sit there, getting ready for some new learning, you may want to give your breath an inspiring color. This color could then move to all parts of your body, filling it. Smiling as it goes in, this color fills and nurtures you.

Let yourself come in touch with your breathing, and feel your self-nurturing through your breath . . .

Now go to that place deep inside yourself and give yourself a message of appreciation. Maybe now you can give yourself permission to let go of all those things you have carried around that are no longer of use. Bid them a fond farewell. Let them go, and be in touch with things you have that fit you well right now. Give yourself permission to add that which you need.

With your message of appreciation to yourself, you can now be ready for whatever you are going to learn today.

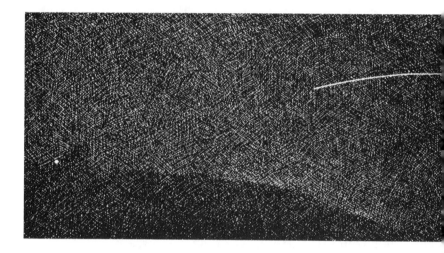

A MESSAGE OF APPRECIATION

Close your eyes and be centered.
Listen to your breathing—
normal, comfortable.
Release the tensions within you.
Just let them escape
on the outgoing breath.
Feel your support, and give yourself
a message of appreciation.
You are a manifestation of life-force—
growing, struggling, sorting, adding.
You can taste everything, but
accept only what fits.

Tune in, focus and
be ready.

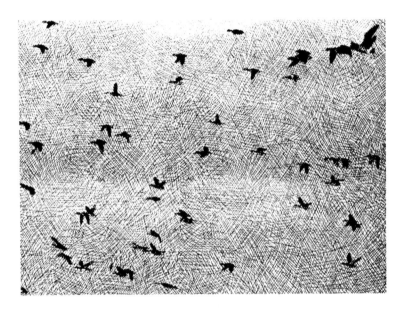

Virginia Satir

Meditations & Inspirations

You HAVE MADE IT

Let yourself become relaxed. Still feeling alert, become aware that, whatever your "trip" has been since you popped out of the womb, *you have made it*. When you are fully aware of that, you can begin to see evidence of it.

Begin now to notice some of the things you learned that may be very helpful to you, some of the things that may be in your way, and some of the things you need but haven't yet learned.

Let your hands come together. Recognize that we all come from the same life-force, equipped with the potential for helping ourselves to become fully evolved. We can all make connections with other people that enrich our lives and enrich theirs, while at the same time honoring our own realities. Using our resources, we deal with whatever comes our way.

Feel the life-force that floats . . .

Let yourself become aware that you are a decision-maker. *You are the one who acts* on the resources you have—your experiences, your hopes, your wishes, your bugs, your worries, your warm fuzzies . . . and no one, but no one else, can be responsible for what you choose to use.

Take a moment to commune with yourself and with the life-force as it floats through your body. Allow yourself a new space to let things unfold. See that you can make decisions about opening and closing at your own request.

Then, very slowly, let your eyes open.

❁

*T*O BE FULLY ME

I need to remember
I am me
and in all the world
there is no one
like me.

I give myself permission
to discover me and use me
lovingly.

I look at myself and see
a beautiful instrument
in which that can happen.

I love me
I appreciate me
I value me.

Taste Everything, Swallow Only That Which Fits

Let your beautiful eyes close. Be aware that your eyelids did what you asked. If you can, notice that it is possible for you to be in touch with all of your body in much the same way. Now, as you're in touch with your eyelids and your body, let your attention go to your breathing. Your breathing depends on you and your awareness, and no one else.

Perhaps as you're in touch with your breathing you can feel it fill your body even more fully. . .

Perhaps at this moment you can give yourself a message that at the time when your body feels stressed, whether there are tears flowing or not, you can remember to be in touch with your breathing. It will allow nurturing in your body, and it will allow you to be in touch with both your humanness and your divinity.

While your eyes are still closed, I'd like you to be aware of the significance of your life, and of the life-force we all have.

Become aware that the ever-present life-force
does not determine what we are to do with life.
We determine that.

When we are children, the people around us are
our main teachers.
Then when we learn
that some of the things our teachers taught us
no longer fit
we can honor our teachers for what they gave us
and go ahead
and learn that which we still need.

We are capable of infinite possibilities and
become limited only when we shut the door on new ones
or when we are not aware
that there are doors we haven't seen.

Virginia Satir   *Meditations & Inspirations*

Breathing

Let yourself come in touch with your breathing. Be aware that it's been going on all the time. Let yourself become aware that the air that goes into your breath is full of oxygen, something your body needs to nurture you. Perhaps now, as you are in touch with your breathing, you can also be in touch with the way your body is taking in breath.

Does it stop at your chest?
Does it go to your abdomen?
Can you feel it in all parts of your body?

Be aware of your breathing. If you feel it is stopping in your chest, give it a gently, loving message and encourage it to go further in your body.

As you get in touch with your breathing and make a closer connection in your awareness between your breath, the nurturing of your body and your heartbeat . . . be aware of how all of your life goes on within you . . . and how you are in charge of making that life in your body more harmonious, richer, and more nurturing. Perhaps now you can allow yourself to be in touch with a part of you that you have not yet acknowledged, like your fingertips or your toes.

Once again be in touch with your breathing. As you breath in, I wonder if you would allow yourself to say the words: "I breath in that which nurtures my beautiful self. I honor the rare person that I am. I give myself full permission to be a whole being. I take on myself the responsibility to enjoy and fulfill my life. When I breath in, I know deep inside of me that my ability to love others, to build with others, to be real with others, to say no or yes, will be enhanced."

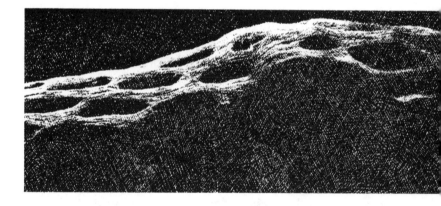

Virginia Satir

Meditations & Inspirations

LIVING YOUR DREAMS

Come in touch with being a child of the universe. To know you are the beneficiary of all the universe has to offer, you need only be able to contact it. To begin, go to that place deep inside yourself where you keep the treasure that is called by your name. Notice all your treasure. Also notice what else you need that you still do not have, and give yourself permission to acquire it.

Dreams and wishes belong together. Dreams and wishes can be manifested. Use the power of a golden wishing wand to make it happen.

Picture your own golden wishing wand in your hand. Endow that wand with the ability to remove your fear of risk-taking. Give it your willingness to go through struggle, to go into something new, to invent that which you need. The golden wand gives you the power to go beyond your own taboos and see new places.

Tarry a moment and look at the golden wishing wand you have created. Feel the texture, look at the form. It's yours, for the rest of your life, to use in whatever way you want.

Greet each day with this nurturing wand.

❀

Virginia Satir

Meditations & Inspirations

THE UNFOLDING OF A NEW DAY

Open a new day
A day which may bring many things
you did not expect
Neither negative nor positive
The day has not yet unfolded.

Allow yourself to
fully take in what
this day will bring.

Give yourself permission to
take only that which fits.

Feel good about your
ability to sort what fits.
No need to feel bad about leaving
that which does not.

You can see that knowledge is
a way of loving
ourselves.

THE LIVING YOU

Be aware that you have energy to use for yourself.
This energy comes from
the center of the earth,
it moves through your feet and legs and
grounds you.

Imagine a color you like and
give it to this energy and
see it move,
floating and swirling in
beautiful circles.

Also be in touch with the energy that comes from
the heavens as it
moves down through your head bringing
inspiration, imagination and visions
of what can be.

As these two energies meet, see them
nurturing each other and
creating a third energy,
the energy of connectedness between
yourself and other beings on this earth.

See this energy moving out
through your arms and hands,
connecting with others when
you hug.
See its color.

Now, see these three colors as
they mingle,
sometimes shading each other,
sometimes adding new dimensions.
Always there, always a fresh supply.

Come in touch with yourself as a
miracle.
There is no one exactly like you
on
the face of the earth.

Go to that place deep within yourself where
you keep that treasure that is called by your name and
as you approach lovingly, gently, excitedly, notice
your resources, your ability to
see, hear, touch, taste, smell, feel, think, move and choose.

Look at what you have now and look forward to
that which you would like to further bring to yourself.
You can do this by allowing your self to
taste all that comes along but
swallow only what fits.

Being Grounded

Go deep inside yourself
Find that treasure that
is known by your name.

Look at this treasure
Look at the resources
that are universal.
You have them all.

You can see
think
hear
feel
taste
smell
choose
move
sort

To *sort*—the ability to
let go of that which once fit
but no longer does, and
see clearly what
fits now.

Now say to yourself,
"I am able,
I can do this.
I have the energy through my
groundedness, my relationship to the heavens,
and my interconnectedness with others.
I am able."

THE DOOR TO YOU

Once again let yourself be in touch with your breathing. Sense your treasurehood. You treasure yourself not only because you're you, but because you are a manifestation of the universal laws of the universe. Recognize that we do not make ourselves, but are co-creators in how we use our selves.

With your mind alert and your body relaxed, I'd like you to become aware of a time and a place when you felt perfectly comfortable. . . a place where you felt in tune with your surroundings, in tune with people (if they were there), with flowers, trees, mountains, and rivers. . . a time and place when you felt perfectly comfortable and everything seemed to be in harmony. I would like you now to give yourself permission to go to that place and again feel the feelings, see the sights, remember the thoughts—experience it all again. Then feel the warmth of the sun, the gentle flow of the wind, the sound of the leaves in the trees, and the colors. You have been in this place many times before.

This time, though, there is something special. It was always there, but you didn't notice until today. It is a door. Something about the door invites you, and you turn towards it, walking gently but firmly with a clear sense of direction. Then you reach into your pocket and discover a shining golden key. As you approach, you pause to observe the door. The door seems to have a handle in exactly the right place. The door seems to be exactly the right height for you to enter comfortably. You insert your golden key into the lock and it fits perfectly. With very little effort you open the door.

As you step through it you are both amazed and not surprised at all. You walk down a few steps into a room that is furnished in your favorite colors. It has your favorite wood trim. The lights are in exactly the right place and of the right intensity. Your favorite music is playing. You stop, immersed in the beauty, amazed at the naturalness of it. Everything is as you like it. Your eyes glow with love for yourself and memories of love for others. You feel excitement at being a part of this world.

Now your eyes go to a bookshelf. The books are well arranged and look inviting. One book catches your eye. It's bound in a special binding. You move towards it, take it from the shelf, and notice that, on the cover, printed exactly as you like, it has your name. For a second you are surprised—but of course, it's natural.

You open the book to the first page and there you read, "The Book of Me." On the next page it begins, "Once upon a time, there was born in . . ." (a certain city, which is your city) and it goes on to describe the events of your life. As you flip through the pages you notice in the chronicle of your life all its efforts, struggles, joys, triumphs, hopes, and fears.

Then you come to the last written page. It carries today's date. Many blank pages follow, and the first of them is entitled "My Life from Now On, Built on the Learnings of Yesterday." As you look at this, you know that all the experiences of yesterday have prepared you for what you have learned differently today.

You take a pen which happens to fit you perfectly and is of exactly the right color, and lovingly, caringly, begin to record your current thoughts and actions. Perhaps more clearly than ever before.

No one ever will read this book except you.

Since this is the first time you consciously write in this way, you write only a short paragraph. However, you promise yourself that you will come back and write whenever you feel like it. You will feel no demand, only an invitation to come back to this rich chronicling, which you do for yourself, in this beautifully bound book.

Feeling of value to yourself, comfortable and good inside, you gently close the book and put it back on the shelf. You know that at any time you can come back to this book.

You turn, pausing to listen to your favorite music. Gently, but with excitement and aliveness, you move across the rich carpet to the door. You step out into a place you have known before. Lock the door and put the golden key into your pocket. Somehow you know that you can never lose this key. It will always be with you.

You come without haste back to a new present, to this room, to this place. Very specifically now, come back to your chair. When you feel like it, let yourself gently open your eyes. Let whatever sounds out that want to come out, and let your body, when it feels like it, move to the music that is now playing.

Virginia Satir

Meditations & Inspirations

*T*HE PREVIOUS NOW

At this moment
experience the previous now.

Look at what you have developed.
Each moment fits you well.

Give yourself permission to
invent that which you need, but
which you do not have.
Depend on your resources. Also,
give yourself permission to
risk something new.

Give yourself permission to
daily, weekly, monthly,
enter into the sorting process.

This can be called
learning or growing or rejoicing.

It can be called
manifesting joyfully your life-force in
your present physical form.

NEW POSSIBILITIES

Give your body a message of love and value.
We have many, many parts to ourselves that are
present, but not manifest . . .
present, but unknown to us . . .
present, but covered up.

So our journey onward,
regardless of where we are,
can always be
a delicious surprise.
Sometimes with pain,
Sometimes with excitement,
But always with new possibilities
for ourselves.

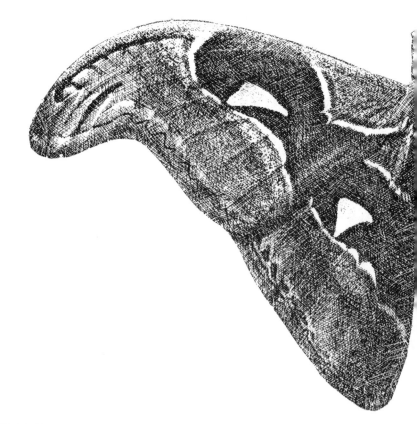

Virginia Satir

Meditations & Inspirations

*H*OW DO YOU FEEL?

Put on a hat that says
I am me
I am whole
I am lovable
I can learn
I can change to what fits for me.

How does that feel?

You who are unique
You who are like everyone
You who are different than everyone

How does that feel?

Look into your mind and
place your hands on your navel.
This is your wholeness.
Remember that you came from two others.

How does that feel?

You can use what you learned from them
You can add what more you need
A process that can go on
for the rest of time.

How does that feel?

Let your body fill with air
You are centered, grounded,
inspired, and connected.
This is with you always.

Feels good.

Connectedness

Very gently, with your eyes closed, explore your skin and all the parts where you can touch. For example feel around the top of your hands, around your fingers, your palms, and your neck. Just explore. As you do this, make little mental notes as to whether you find wetness or dryness, hardness or softness, or whatever is there. Just let yourself explore.

As you are exploring, let yourself be aware of any thoughts or feelings that might dance through your head or your stomach. Now, deepen your touch by letting yourself feel *under* the skin. This brings you in touch with the flow of your blood and, deeper down, the movement of your muscles. It's as if you add a little power to the movement and are saying, "This is what's under skin. The ability to move, to support, to hang on, to lift, to pleasure." Let yourself know what you are thinking and feeling as this goes on.

Very gently and very slowly, find your pulse. It can be located in your fingertips. If you can't find it there, look for it in your wrist. Now you are in touch with your heartbeat. As you become aware of your heartbeat, let yourself feel the rhythm, the ebb and flow. At the point when you can definitely feel this rhythm, let your breathing be in the same rhythm. Breathe in the same rhythm that your heart is beating for a few breaths. As you are in touch with your breathing and your heartbeat, let yourself be in touch with your own feelings of yourself.

Could you also let yourself know that you are supporting yourself with your own body? Mostly you are using your bottom, or your back, or your feet. You are supporting you. You are in touch with you. Let yourself know what you are feeling about that. Let yourself know that you can feel this way at any time; you don't need someone to do this for you. You carry you with you at all times.

Slowly move your hands apart and rest your chin in them, so that the palms of your hands are under your chin and your fingers hug your cheeks. Let you rest in you. Let yourself be aware that your hands are holding you. What does it feel like to have this exquisite, alive support and connection? Letting your hands take all of the weight, see if your hands can really support your head. Once again, let yourself be in touch with your breathing. You can support you. You can contact you. You can nurture you.

Let your hands, very gently and slowly, reach the skin and have a meeting, a contact. Whatever your hands can find, your lips, your forehead, make a meeting with your skin. As you are doing this, pick a time when you can do this with your whole body. Very slowly and very gently, let your hands come to rest somewhere on you. Perhaps, at this time, you can allow yourself the thought, "I am in touch with my feelings and being. My most precious possession is mine. I can love it. I can guide it. I can improve it. I can hear it. I can see it. I can change it and I can own it. It's the only thing in the world I can fully own. It's always available to me. I'm never without it." Now, just let yourself be in touch with what feelings flow as these thoughts come to your awareness.

❀

YOUR TREASUREHOOD

Feel your treasurehood.
The miracle that you are
not only because you are you
but because you are a manifestation
of the universal laws

of
the
UNIVERSE

We do not make ourselves.
We are only co-creators.

Love yourself,
for you are
a member of
the universe.

*Y*OUR BODY WORKS

Let yourself take in your breath.
Be aware that you are taking in nutrients
for your body.
By your will
By your direction
By your physiology,
with thousands of beautiful canals
inside your body.
Let your body be filled
with your breath.

YOUR CONTROL TOWER

Let yourself be aware of the miracle! You just wish, you just think, and those beautiful eyelids close. Could you be in just such an intimate relationship with the rest of your body? Now let yourself become aware of your breathing, just aware of it, feeling it coming in, knowing that it brings healthy oxygen to your body . . . feeling all those parts of yourself that are especially designed to give the air a way to get to all of your body. Perhaps today you can give it some gentle encouragement to move throughout your body, and if in this journey the oxygen comes to some little tight places, acknowledge them, release them and bless them, especially for letting you know that they were uncomfortable.

Now, at this moment, feel yourself centered. Your body on the chair, your feet on the floor, your back against the chair. Extend the feeling of centeredness throughout the room, the building, the city or town, the surrounding countryside, the nation, the North American continent, the Western Hemisphere . . . cross both oceans and encompass all the countries on the planet, still centered here, you in the center of the universe. As you do that, let yourself become aware that we are all manifestations of life-force.

Perhaps we can get into the shoes of astronaut Ed Mitchell who, when he was in outer space, hid the whole planet behind his thumb. He has said that was the moment when he knew that all life was the same and that our planet was small and fragile, but that it represented the universe. He could see the planet in that perspective and at the same time remember himself being in a certain space (like you are now) aware of only what was around him. It would be easy to forget that the other perspective was there. I call that outer-space position, the airport control-tower position. From there we can view the whole, and at the same time appreciate the specific, while knowing we are all alike, only in varying forms.

ENERGY AND FREEDOM

Energy is for support
of
the human soul
as
it moves toward its freedom.

Freedom and its manifestation
is
the kind of perfection
we
are all destined to have.

Virginia Satir   Meditations & Inspirations

*T*OGETHERNESS

Be as aware as you can, of being with these people
at this moment,
Just being with them.
Be aware of whatever

thoughts
feelings
connections

move through your head
relative to these people

Be aware of what's relative to
the whole way we look at families

And relative to the phenomenon
of what it means to be fully human.

Be in touch with this, because
this is the resource of your learning.

Virginia Satir   Meditations & Inspirations

WITH ONE ANOTHER

Let your eyes close.
Be in touch with your breathing,
your body alert yet relaxed.
Slowly take each others' hands and
feel the energy flowing, not through one,
through three.
Be in touch with the life-force of three people;
feel the force flow.
You are part of this group.
You are loved and beloved, an
important member of this universe.

A *NEW PRESENT*

It is the human situation to meet the present with interpretations of the past.

The meaning of the present is to allow us to leave the past and see the Now in its own right.

Experience will soon become your past and a foundation for a new present and future.

Virginia Satir

Meditations & Inspirations

YOUR RIVER FLOWS FREELY

At this moment I'd like you to be in touch with your breathing. If you find any little tensions within your body, release them on the outgoing breath. Be aware of your energy coming from the center of the earth, coming from the heavens, coming from your contacts with other people. Feel all that energy blending within you. And again, be in touch with your breathing. Perhaps you can make a mental note to check periodically on your breathing.

Now, go to the part of yourself that contains your memory. As you meet that part, go back in time to when you first had your experiences, to when you first remember your life. Go back in your memory and see if you recall the feelings and, remembering them, feel them again. Then let yourself advance in your memory.

Virginia Satir

Meditations & Inspirations

Remember when you started putting together the pieces of what you wanted from this life on earth. Remember the feelings you had as you participated in the building of your own context and own activities. What did that feel like for you? If you had any doubts or concerns then, perhaps you can feel them again now. No demand, just a possibility. Staying at this point, ask your memory to help you recall what it was you hoped for in this life. Specifically remember what you wanted, and then ask your memory to move along and come up to the present.

Was there a connection between what you hoped for and what you got so far? Consult your self. As you went through the process of trying to get what you hoped for, did anything else turn up? Did any other things turn up that you saw as interesting or beckoning? Did you add to your excitement, to your intelligence, to your life-force?

At this point, do you have any questions or things that puzzle you? As you think of them, perhaps a link will come to you and you will make connections. Give yourself permission to ask those questions that might provide those links and help you make the connections. Perhaps you could, at this moment, create a mental picture. On your right are an assortment of pieces that seem to belong together. On your left is another assortment of pieces that also seem to fit together. Imagine that there might be a link between your left and your right. A way of stringing together all of the pieces. Maybe that's what your questions could be about.

Now, just breathe normally. Breathe comfortably, normally, letting your body, your mind, your heart, feel what's going on. Go to that place inside yourself where your appreciation button is and give it a little touch. See what music it gives you now. How does it feel to touch your appreciation button and say, "I appreciate me."

As you breathe comfortably and normally, notice if there are any body responses coming. Is there something letting go, something tightening, something getting juicy, something getting dry, or whatever? Know that this is only a response to what you are doing right now. It is not the oncoming of a great disease. It is only a response coming out of yourself. It is from your thoughts, your feelings, your memories, your body, your self-worth, your appreciation.

As you are breathing normally and comfortably, feeling contentment in your body. Let yourself be aware that you are unique. This means that you are like everyone else in some basic ways, and you are different from everyone else in many, many ways. All this added up makes you unique. There is no duplicate.

I'd like you to be aware of what you have discovered about how you are different from the others and how you are the same. Be aware of how you struggled to make connections and what the outcomes of successful struggling were. Recall the ebb and flow as things moved. Again, be aware of your breathing, be in touch with what's happening to you at this point. Breathing comfortably, allow yourself to become aware that it is the human situation to meet the present with interpretations of the past. The meaning of the present is to allow the present to leave the past, and be seen in its right.

If there are some puzzles, some things you would like to connect, to feel more complete in your experience, allow yourself to come into contact with those things. Think of completing—not ending—*completing.* Be aware that one way of completing is to acknowledge that it is not complete. Some things take a long time to complete, and that's OK.

Once again, be aware of your breathing. Breathe normally and comfortably. I would like you to cup your hands and place them right in front of your navel. As you do this, feel in your hands that you have been aware of giving. Feel what it does to your whole body to do that. Feel what you are feeling.

Now, at a certain point, let your hands again form a cup. Bring it to yourself, adding fully to yourself. This is the process of giving, taking, expanding, letting go, adding to; it can go on for the rest of your life. Be sure that your shoulders are relaxed. For a moment match the rhythm of your breathing. Let yourself be in touch with the feelings inside of you at this moment.

Let your right hand rest on your left wrist or vice versa. Be in touch with your heartbeat. Feel the ebb and flow. This is your own firsthand evidence of your own life-force, which is housed in that beautiful miracle of a body. It's in there with all of your parts: your mind, your emotions, your sense, your interactions with other people, your context and your source of life.

Let yourself know that at any time, under any conditions, you can connect with your life-force. You only need to remember that you can be in immediate touch with your link to yourself and the universe.

Now, for a few moments only, could you pace the rhythm of your breathing to the pace of your own heartbeat. Feel the evidence of your own life-force. You'll also be aware of your support. Your feet, your back, your bottom, available to you whenever you choose.

As you get ready to close this experience, remember the seat of your own power. This power is your self, your worth, your ability to connect with whomever you choose. Let yourself become fully relaxed. Let your hands rest wherever they feel comfortable.

Virginia Satir

Meditations & Inspirations

MY FAREWELL

Let yourself become fully aware of your breathing. Let yourself be aware of the nurturing elements of your breathing. And maybe today, more than any time before, you can be aware that you did not invent your breath, that you did not invent the vehicle by which the breath goes in. All you do is invent the pace, the amount, the direction your breath takes. This is a big gift for you. *You are in charge.* The air and your mechanism for handling it is there. You only have to put it together.

In this same metaphor, love is all around. You have the capacity and the machinery for utilizing and experiencing love. You only have to put it together.

Energy is all around. You have the equipment to process the energy. Your only need to bring the energy and the different uses for it to yourself.

Your self-worth is everywhere. Everyone has their own. You have the machinery, the equipment, to live it. All you have to do is bring the source of it together with your direction and handling.

It is the same with everything else. You are the one who brings together the source with your beautiful body, mind and heart, and finds the uses. Wouldn't it be an immense jump for you to have to invent all the energy as well as to invent the means by which to use it? But you only have to use it, not invent it. You have to keep your eyes on the uses. That may not be very much, but for some of us it's a whole lifetime's work.

Once again, let yourself be in touch with your breathing. Remind yourself that, by the very fact that you are present on this planet, you are privy to the energy coming to you from the center of the earth. All you have to do is be aware of it; it's always there. It is the energy of groundedness that comes from that center upward through your feet and legs. It's like the energy of the heavens, which is always there and comes to you down through your head, face, neck and arms to join with the energy of groundedness. That energy from the heavens is the energy of inspiration, of sensing, and of feeling one with all life. Accept that beautiful energy of inspiration and groundedness; let them come together and create still a third energy. This is the energy of connectedness with fellow human beings.

Let yourself go to that beautiful place deep inside yourself where you find the resources that allow you to use this energy of inspiration, connectedness, and groundedness. This is your ability to see, not only with your physical eyes, but also behind your physical eyes. This is your ability to hear the sounds of words and of music, the music of laughing and the agony of crying. Also the ability to hear, behind the physical ear, to what is intended. This is your ability to touch, taste and smell and to touch behind the touch, to smell behind the smell. This is also your ability to speak, to put thought into words—to use that grand evolver of words, your left brain. It has these beautiful codes and definitions, the ability to do mathematics, to analyze and to rationalize. And to use the other side, your right brain, which gives you your juices, your awareness, and your joy or pain in living.

You are a veritable storehouse, running twenty-four hours a day, creating thoughts—some of them useful, some of them foolish. And you have a choice out of all of that material that you are creating to choose what you want to use now. Marvelous, isn't it?

You also have the ability to move. What a beautiful resource. You can move those 206 bones connected with many, many fibers of muscle. And then there are more beautiful systems. The blood system, your air system, your cooling and warming system, your central nervous system, your autonomic nervous system.

You are filled with treasures that help you to move and to move into awareness. Movement is life, and you have movement and life.

You have the ability to sort out of yesterday what fits for today. You know that you can keep and evolve that which is left over from yesterday but which no longer fits today. You can bless it because it was a big part of getting you to where you are today. Accept that the price has become too high to continue using the old ways. Look again at what you have now and then look ahead, knowing that you have the resources to meet the future.

Remind yourself that you have a golden key that admits you to a sanctuary all your own. It is decorated in your favorite colors, designed in your favorite style, and contains your favorite books and music. Remember your wishing stick, the golden wand that gives you the power to translate your wishes and the courage to state them. Without wishes being stated nothing can happen. When they are stated, things can happen. And when you invite others to be part of your wish-fulfillment, even more can happen. Remember the wishing stick that gives you courage in the face of fear, that allows you to come in touch with what you are feeling and thinking.

Introduce yourself to your medallions. Imagine them hanging on a beautifully crafted pendant which has "no" on one side and "yes" on the other. They give you the ability to say "Yes, it does fit" or "No, it doesn't fit right now." This yes and no allows you to keep in touch with where you are in the present moment. Remember, it's based on fit. "It doesn't fit now, but if may fit later." But the important thing is, does it fit now?

Now you are armed with your golden key, your wishing stick and your yes/no medallions.

You are armed with your ability to be aware of and direct your breathing in order to be in touch with your physical self.

You are armed with your caring and loving, your emotional self, your intellectual self.

You are armed with your interactional self, that I/Thou part.

You are armed with your sensual self, where all the holes become *wholes,* and with your nutritional self, which controls everything you put into yourself.

You are armed with your contextual self, which is your relationship to light and sound, to air and temperature, to time, space and color.

You are armed with your spiritual self, which connects you with the whole universe where the real plan for how we can become exists.

You do not have a limited destiny. Rather, you have the energy and abilities to fulfill the beautiful human map, the beautiful human self.

As I leave you now, I leave you with tears—tears of joy that I've had this time with you. I see on the horizon more love, more relevance, more real cooperation, and I thank you for having joined me in this way. Now, when you are ready, say goodbye to what we've had and hello to what can happen.

Farewell.

JOHN BANMEN

An author, researcher, therapist and educator, he has been an Associate Professor at the University of British Columbia, in the Department of Counseling Psychology, since 1979.

He is President of the B.C. Association of Marriage and Family Therapy and past president of the Canadian Guidance and Counseling Association.

He is a frequent workshop leader in British Columbia and has a private practice in family therapy.

JANE GERBER

She is a member of the Satir/Avanta Network Governing Council for 1985–1988. Jane is a psychotherapist in private practice in Evanston, Illinois; co-founder of Oasis-Midwest Training Center; Founding Fellow and Senior faculty member of the Gestalt Institute of Chicago.

A long time colleague of Virginia Satir, Jane has done numerous workshops throughout the United States, Canada, Mexico, England and Japan.

VIRGINIA SATIR

The late Virginia Satir authored *Peoplemaking* and *Conjoint Family Therapy,* both are considered classics on family dynamics. Other popular books by Virginia Satir are: *Self Esteem, Making Contact* and *Your Many Faces.* She also co-authored *Helping Families to Change* and *Changing with Families.*

VIRGINIA SATIR
MEDITATIONS ON VIDEO

BOOKS & POSTERS BY VIRGINIA SATIR

MAKING CONTACT by Virginia Satir shows how you can better understand the basic tools for making contact with others and explains how you can use them to work for change in your perceptions, your actions, and your life. 96 pages, soft cover, $6.95.

In *SELF ESTEEM* Virginia Satir presents an essential credo for the individual in modern society. This classic poem, beautifully illustrated, is a simple and succinct declaration of self-worth. 64 pages, soft cover, $4.95.

YOUR MANY FACES offers Virginia Satir's central theme developed in more than 40 years as therapist, author, lecturer and consultant. She demonstrates that your many faces reveal the real you and she helps you accept them as the key to opening the door to new opportunities. 128 pages, soft cover, $6.95

The *I AM ME* poster is Virginia Satir's declaration of self-esteem, stating in part, that "In all the world there is no one else exactly like me and everything that comes out of me is authentically mine because I alone chose it . . ." 23″ × 35″, full color, $3.95.

THE FIVE FREEDOMS poster offers the freedom to "see and hear," "say," "feel," "ask," and "take risks" and Virginia Satir explains how to see and hear, say, feel, ask, and take risks for a better you. 35″ × 23″, full color, $3.95.

On the *PEOPLE ARE MIRACLES* poster, beautifully illustrated with the silhouette of a ballerina, Virginia Satir's words are printed . . . "People need to see themselves as basic miracles and worthy of love." 23″ × 35″, full color, $3.95.

The *MAKING CONTACT* poster delineates Virginia Satir's belief of what is the greatest gift one can conceive of having from anyone and what is the greatest gift one can give to someone. 23″ × 35″, full color, $3.95.

Virginia Satir offers *GOALS,* a poster providing the answer to loving, appreciating, joining, inviting, having, criticizing, and helping one another and thereby enriching one another. 23″ × 35″, full color, $3.95.

To order, send check or money order to:
> Celestial Arts
> P.O. Box 7327
> Berkeley, CA 94707
> Attn: Retail Dept.

Please add the correct postage & handling required for your order.

Posters   **(UPS)** 1–5 posters, add $2.25. For each additional poster add 50¢.

Books   **(4th class)** For one book add $1.00. For each additional book add 50¢.

(UPS) For one book add $2.25. For each additional book add 50¢.

California residents add your local sales tax.